SECRETS
OF THE
RAINFOREST

Carron Brown

Illustrated by Alyssa Nassner

Ivy Kids

A rainforest is bustling with life.

If you look closely at each tree
through branches, vines and ferns,
and around the huge roots, you will
spot the animals living there.

Shine a torch behind the page,
or hold it up to the light to reveal
what is hidden in and around one
tree. Discover a small world
of great surprises.

Rainforest trees grow tall with wide trunks and long roots.

Can you see one very tall tree in the forest?

Creak!

The tree has many
branches near its top.

Sunlight hits the
leaves there.

Many flying creatures rest high up on the sunny leaves.

What's hiding under this leaf?

A beautiful butterfly is resting.

His open wings are larger than
both your hands put together.

Flutter...

Flutter...

Suddenly, the butterfly flutters into the air.

Other butterflies take off around the treetop.

Who could have startled them?

Whoosh!

A spider monkey is swinging
through the trees. Her strong tail
clings to branches and vines.

Some plants grow on the tree's branches. Their leaves catch raindrops.

Can you see who lives in this colourful plant?

Splash!

A tree frog and his tadpole
live in a pool of water inside the plant.

Soon, the tadpole will become a frog.

The treetop is a safe place to build a home. It's far away from dangerous animals on the ground.

Who waits in this large nest?

This large chick is
a young harpy eagle.
Her parents fly to
the nest to feed her.

Squawk!
Squawk!

Golden lion tamarins
scurry from branch to branch.
They are looking for
tasty insects or fruit to eat.

What are they carrying?

Chatter!
Chatter!

zzz   zzz   zzz

Baby monkeys ride piggyback.
They're too young to travel alone.

Long, thin vines hang in
a tangle around the tree.
Creatures climb
the woody stalks.

Who looks
like a vine?

A parrot snake is smelling
by sticking out his tongue.

He uses it to sense
food and danger.

Sssssslither!

Most animals race along the tops of the branches. Others take their time.

Can you spot an upside-down creature?

Yawn!

A sloth moves very slowly.
Algae grows on her fur

It turns her coat green.

Colourful flowers bloom in the rainforest. Animals see their bright shapes.

Who drinks from this red flower?

Whirr!

Hummingbirds
hover by beating
their wings very fast.

Their long tongues
sip sugary liquid
from flowers.

Leafy ferns cover
the ground by the tree.
They make a perfect
place to hide.

Can you see who's
waiting to pounce?

roar!

A jaguar is a big cat
that eats other animals.

He has sharp teeth and claws.

There are more insects than any other
type of animal in the rainforest.

Can you count the leaf-carrying insects?

Snip!

Snip!

A trail of leafcutter ants
are marching to their nest.
The leaves are used to
make food for young ants.

Fallen branches create
homes for plants and animals.

Can you see who is
inside this plant?

Slurp!

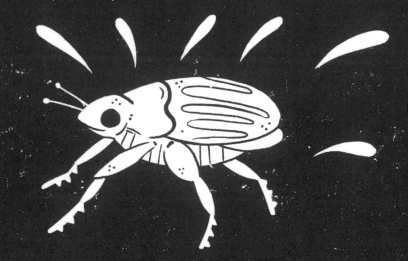

A beetle is trapped inside the slimy walls of a sun pitcher. This plant eats small animals.

A salamander
has spotted danger
lurking in a hollow.

What has he spied
beneath the rock?

A big wandering spider waits
to leap out and catch prey
with one poisonous bite.

Pounce!

There's a
well-trodden path
around the tree.

Can you spot who's
walking this way?

Snuffle...
Snuffle...

A tapir is heading to the river for a swim.
Her long nose snatches up leaves
to eat along the way.

The river runs through the rainforest.

Who is making bubbles?

Swish...
Swoosh...

A pink river dolphin uses his large
flippers to swim. He hunts fish, crabs
and turtles in the water.

As night falls,
the animals who were
busy during the day
fall asleep.

But the rainforest is never quiet.
In the evening, the night-time
animals wake up. Hundreds of
shining eyes catch the
fading light.

There's more...

Half of all the plants and animals in the world live in rainforests.
There's life everywhere you look.

In the upper canopy The top branches get the most sunlight. Winged creatures such as eagles, parrots, butterflies and bats, and climbing animals such as monkeys, reach these dizzy heights.

Climbing down The canopy is a tangle of leaves and branches. Rain drips off the leaves, watering flowers and fruits. Many animals live in this food-rich place, including monkeys, sloths, snakes and tree frogs.

Lower levels It's darker near the bottom of the tree. But enough sunlight finds a way through the branches for plants such as ferns. Hummingbirds feed on flowers and monkeys climb on the vines.

Roots Large rainforest trees can have huge roots, called buttress roots, that help prop them up. The roots take up water from the soil to help the tree grow. They also take goodness from decaying leaves on the ground.

On the ground

Dead leaves and twigs make the forest floor a great place for creepy-crawlies to live, with lots of places to hide and decaying plants to eat. Tapirs feed on the shoots of new plants that stretch up to the sunlight.

In the river

Many creatures live in the river that winds through the forest, including river dolphins, piranha fish, turtles and caimans. Capybara (the largest rodent), giant otters and anaconda snakes live both on the land and in the river.

Inside plants

Spiky plants called bromeliads live on tree branches. Rainwater falls onto their leaves and runs down into a pool in the centre of the plant. Some tree frogs carry their tadpoles to a bromeliad pool where they grow into adult frogs.

Deadly plants

Pitcher plants send out sweet smells that attract insects. Once the creature climbs into the main part of the plant, it cannot get out because the surface is too slippery. The trapped insect is eventually eaten by the plant.

Night-time

By 6pm the forest is dark. There are some animals that are awake only at night. Owls, bats, moths, spiders and many more creatures start looking for food. Frogs croak, crickets chirrup, monkeys howl and birds screech – night-time is very noisy!

First published in the UK in 2014 by

Ivy Press

210 High Street

Lewes

East Sussex BN7 2NS

United Kingdom

www.ivypress.co.uk

ISBN: 978-1-78240-149-0

This book was conceived, designed & produced by

Ivy Press

CREATIVE DIRECTOR Peter Bridgewater

MANAGING EDITOR Hazel Songhurst

COMMISSIONING EDITOR Georgia Amson-Bradshaw

SENIOR EDITOR Jacqui Sayers

ART DIRECTOR Kim Hankinson

DESIGNER Glyn Bridgewater

Printed in China

Origination by Ivy Press Reprographics

10 9 8 7 6 5 4 3 2 1

MIX
Paper from
responsible sources
FSC® C016973

FSC
www.fsc.org